BIRDS COLORING BOOK FOR KIDS 4 TO 8

Different Types of Birds Names

DUCK

PEAFOWL

TURKEY

PARROT

OSTRICH

CHICKEN

EAGLE

TOUCAN

KIWI

PIGEON

PENGUIN

OWL

STORK

FROGMOUTH

DUCK   PEAFOWL   TURKEY   PARROT

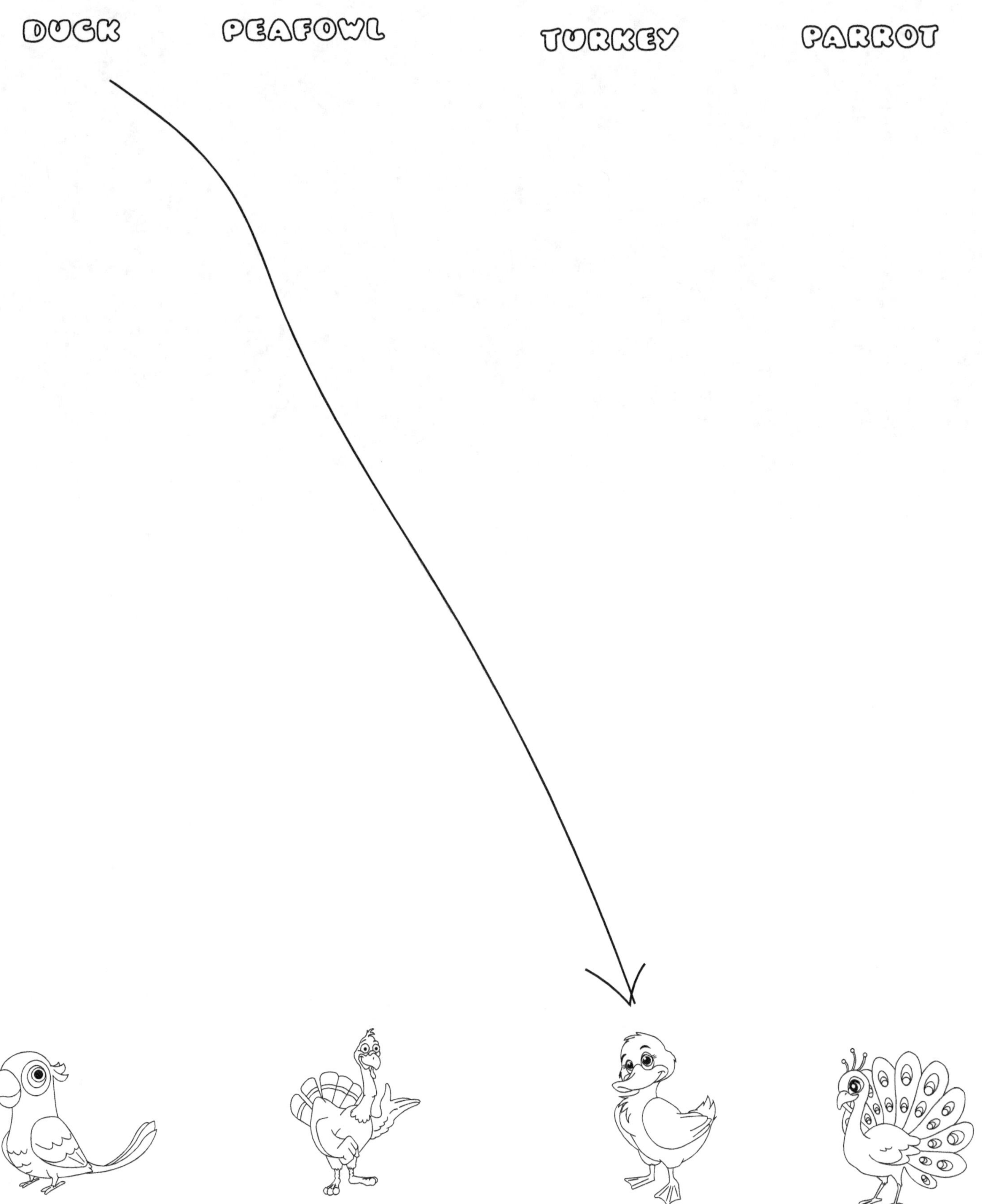

OSTRICH   CHICKEN   EAGLE   TOUCAN

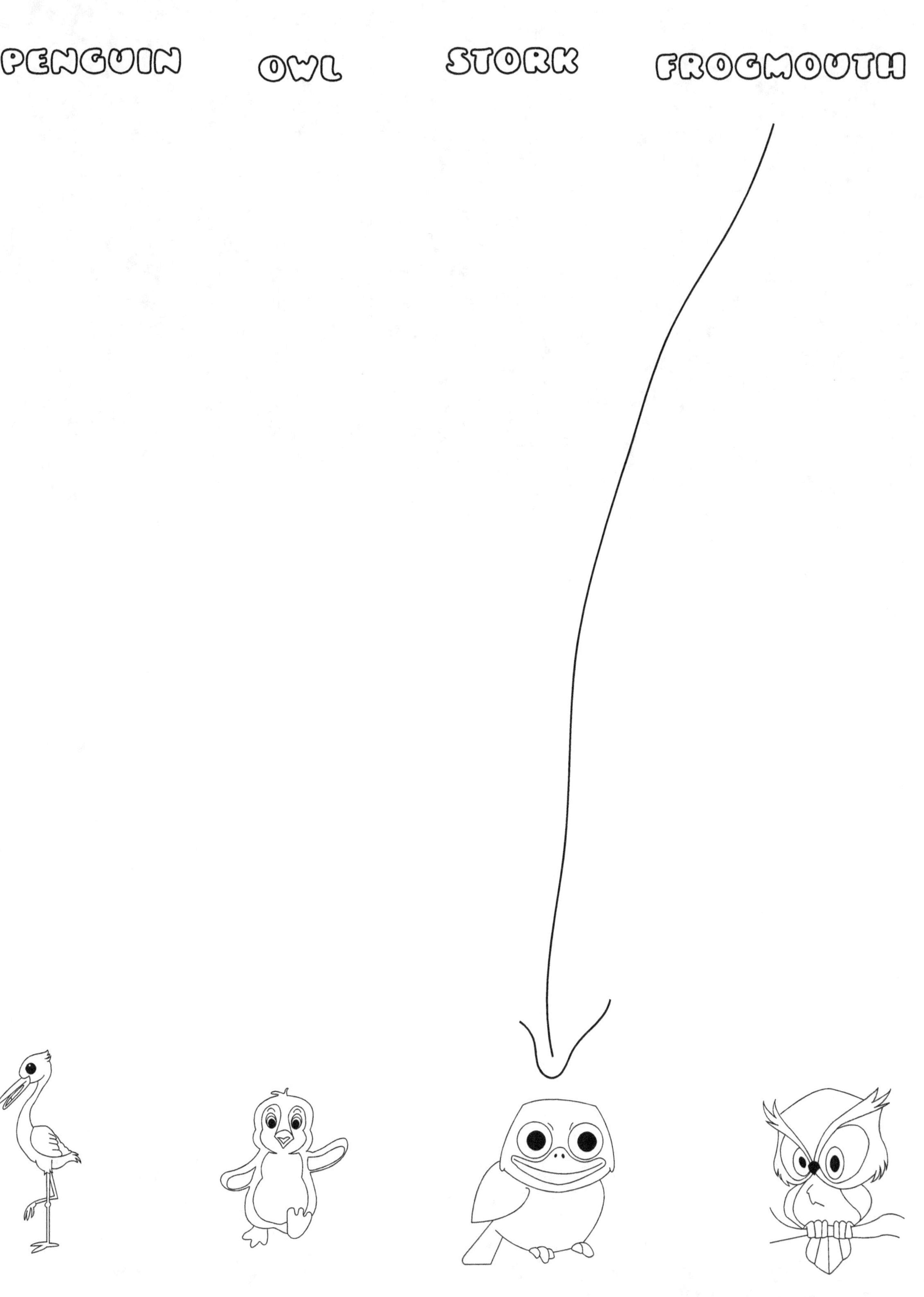

PENGUIN
OWL
STORK
FROGMOUTH

KIWI   PIGEON

DUCK

CHICKEN

PENGUIN

PEAFOWL

EAGLE

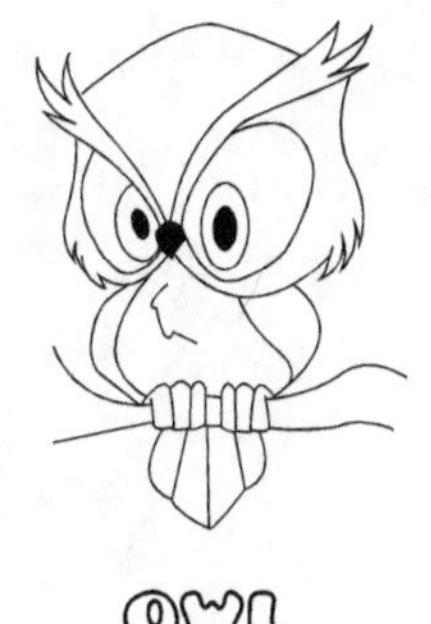

OWL

TURKEY

TOUCAN

STORK

PARROT

KIWI

FROGMOUTH

OSTRICH

PIGEON

* 9 7 9 8 5 8 4 4 4 7 3 5 9 *